RETIREMENT
So you *think* you can retire?

The myths and realities
you might want to consider before
embarking on this new phase of life
that you *think* can only be better.

Wendy L Yacura

Retirement … So you think you can retire?
Copyright © 2018 by Wendy L Yacura

All rights reserved. No part of this publication
may be reproduced, distributed, or transmitted
in any form or by any means, including
photocopying, recording, or other electronic
or mechanical methods, without the prior
written permission of the author, except in the
case of brief quotations embodied in critical
reviews and certain other non-commercial uses
permitted by copyright law.

Tellwell Talent
www.tellwell.ca

ISBN
978-0-2288-0091-0 (Paperback)
978-0-2288-0092-7 (eBook)

TABLE OF CONTENTS

Dedication i
Introduction iii

Chapter 1
The Decision to Retire 1

Chapter 2
RRSPs in Retirement 6

Chapter 3
Housing 10

Chapter 4
The Financial Collapse in 2008.................. *14*

Chapter 5
Recovery After 10 Years *17*

Chapter 6
Financial Markets Now *22*

Chapter 7
Senior Helping Seniors.......................... *28*

Chapter 8
Senior Housing Facilities........................ *31*

Chapter 9
Finding Balance *36*

Chapter 10
What's Really Important? *39*

References *46*
Glossary..................................... *47*
About the Author *48*

DEDICATION

My wish for you, my children and grandchildren, is to develop the personal strength and vivacity to prepare yourself for the journey to retirement, because without these components, retirement could be challenging and not the "golden" years we so often hear about.

Love you to the moon and back and wish you the utmost in health, happiness, and financial stability.

INTRODUCTION

DID I RETIRE TOO SOON? MANY OF US MAY FIND OURSELVES ASKING this question years down the road when we realize how much money we have spent and how many years we can expect to live. Granted, many have perhaps not been quite as fortunate to be able to make that choice for a number of reasons. Particularly in these times, the decision may have been made for you. Perhaps you were forced into retirement at a point in your life when you may not have been totally prepared to enter that phase. Your health may have been a factor, which I can only imagine would be a difficult and frightening decision to have to make.

For most, I hope retirement is an exciting time after many years of work and raising a family. It now saddens me to think that many of us express how we can't wait for retirement. That might be all you hear from someone who is nearing their retirement phase. I find myself reminding younger friends and family to enjoy those working years and paycheques, because you will never have that opportunity again. David Chilton writes in The Wealthy Barber, "Your years in retirement should be among the best years of your life. So you owe it to yourself to do everything possible now to enable you to enjoy fully those later years. That means saving enough money in your working years to enable you to maintain your income in retirement." I, for one, was guilty of talking about retirement, and yet I never really had enough working pensionable years. Thinking back now, I was naïve, as I expect many of us are. It may be a matter of age and expectation.

As we get on in our lives, we slow down and get tired, knowing very well we cannot continue in the workforce forever. We then start thinking of our options and begin to plan for the next chapter. We almost feel an entitlement to it. After many years of hard work and often a few hardships, that is totally reasonable. But do we really know how much money we need? Have we actually taken all the necessary steps to ensure there will be enough funds to last into our final days? How will we spend all that spare time? For those of you who have found the answers and are fortunate to have excellent health, I expect retirement will be a wonderful experience for you.

Today, many companies in Canada do not provide a pension. They may offer a retirement savings plan (RSP), which from what I understand does not compare to a defined pension plan (DPP). A DPP, according to Wikipedia, is a type of pension plan in which a employer/sponsor promises a specified pension payment, lump sum (or combination of) on retirement that is predetermined by a formula based on the employee's earning history, tenure of service and age, rather than depending directly on individual investment returns. A defined benefit plan is "defined" in the sense that the benefit formula is defined and known in advance. Conversely, for a "defined contribution retirement saving plan," the formula for computing the employer's and employee's contributions is defined and known in advance, but the benefit to be paid out is not known in advance.

According to 2008 figures from Statistics Canada, taken directly from the RetirementAdvisor.ca website, "only 38% of paid workers had a company-sponsored pension plan as part of their compensation. For those who are covered, the two main types of company pension are the Defined Benefit pension plan and the Defined Contribution pension plan."

I cannot speak to the American system. I never really understand Suze Orman when she refers to the Roth IRA and 401k and any other US company pension plans, so I am unable to make any reference to their system. I am happy I am not a US resident dependent on what they may or may not offer. What benefits does a US citizen have in retirement anyway? We all know the state of chaos their health care system is in with Donald Trump now in power, and what does that mean for a retiree? In fact, just this week, the hosts on The View stated that health care is available to all seniors. I suppose that for seniors in the United States, the expense of health care is not an issue. I still don't think I care to be a citizen there. This is the time when we may need the health care system more than ever, and we need to feel secure enough to know that the system is there when and if you need it. Chances are, we will in our golden years need the system to be a good one, as I expect most of us will become increasingly dependent on health care because of the complications and risk factors as we age. We need to stay healthy and take responsibility for our health and well being, although that may become more challenging as we age.

Suffice it to say, I am happy to be a Canadian retiree. Retirement offers new and different challenges, and I know there are many retirees with very active and social lifestyles who are healthy and financially secure. That's the model of retirement. It doesn't always work out that way. Some of us baby boomers may be finding retirement more of an

Introduction

adjustment than our parents did. Many of our parents, as mine did, led a much simpler lifestyle and managed to hold on to one job throughout their entire careers. This is almost unheard of now. Many have had to jump ship and even change careers due to downsizing, restructuring, and companies going bankrupt. This may have been a financial burden and strain on their retirement plans, and they may be working well into their 60s and 70s.

How will our children survive retirement if they are unable to make a good wage or salary? What are the chances they will have any kind of pension, let alone company pension? Will they be able to collect from the Canada Pension Plan (CPP)? It wasn't too long ago I was talking to my son about finances and retirement, and he said there's no guarantee the average person will even be able to collect from a company pension due to closures and bankruptcies—for example, Stelco. Who would have ever thought these pensioners would have their pensions and benefits compromised? Sears is going down, and many employees are in jeopardy of losing their pensions and possibly benefits. In my opinion it is simply criminal that this is a reality for so many Hamiltonians. We all know a family member or friend who has worked for either company. To know that their pensions and financial security are in limbo and even in jeopardy is just so wrong. The average person or family has only so many financial resources to turn to, and when they're gone, then what?

My sister inspired me the other day to write about retirement. She works in the financial markets and has helped me invest and encouraged me to balance my money conservatively, particularly in retirement. However, retirement has not been an easy transition. Although I love the flexibility of retirement (doing what I want when I want is completely wonderful), I'm not so sure I have adapted well to managing on what is often referred to as a fixed income. I loathe hearing that. After many years of working and raising a family, saving, budgeting, and limited vacations, now that we're in our last phase of life, we have to survive on fixed incomes?

In this book I plan to write about the myths and realities of retirement from my perspective as a woman living alone and retiring at a relatively young but healthy age of 62. Little did I know I would feel this way after seven and a half years of retirement. It's been fun, but I feel many frustrations, which have resulted in my aspiration to write about them. If anything, as a reader you may make an educated and informed decision to retire at a time when you are ready to transition into a new phase—one you will hopefully be able to reflect upon positively, knowing it was the best time for you. Clearly I don't have all the answers, but I do have many opinions, which you may or may not agree with, and that's okay. That's the privilege we have as Canadians. We are able to enjoy democracy, and in some parts of the world that has yet to be achieved. I expect that in developing countries, retirement is unheard of. It may only be a word and one that unfortunately many may never realize.

Chapter 1
THE DECISION TO RETIRE

AS YOU MOVE INTO YOUR RETIREMENT WINDOW, GATHER AS MUCH information and advice as you can to ensure you are well positioned not only financially but emotionally as well. It is a huge adjustment, and more often than not, very few of us want to go back in time. It is an emotional adjustment because for many years we felt we had a purpose and were contributing to something at work every day. Upon retirement, that comes to a sudden halt. As for myself, had I not chosen to retire in January 2011, I would have returned to work on January 2 after the holidays. On that day and pretty much for that entire week, I was depressed. I found myself questioning whether I had made the right decision. I could have continued working for an additional five years on a new grant, which was an extension to an international follow-up project I had been working on. I knew at 62 I could not work another five years in a high-energy and high-demand environment. I turned down that opportunity, and I found myself second-guessing my decision, *albeit only for one week.*

If you are fortunate to have 30 or more pensionable years, and even better if you have a DPP, you may appear to be in good shape. If your DPP happens to be indexed to inflation, doubly better. If I may reference David Chilton in his book The Wealthy Barber, "Many pensions are not adjusted each year to reflect the rising costs of living, that is, they are not indexed. Others are not fully indexed. They may have a cap of a four or eight percent annual increase in benefits. If inflation were to hover at 10 percent for a number of years, the receivers of non-indexed or partially indexed pensions could find themselves in trouble. Hundreds of thousands of people were caught in this bind in the early eighties."

You may have contributed to registered retirement savings plans (RRSPs) as well as a tax-free savings account (TFSA). And if your house is paid for, you should be set, barring any major unforeseen circumstances. You may even have other investments or real estate properties, which will position you even more comfortably. This might sound like the ideal situation to be in, but I wonder how many are well positioned financially in these times. Sometimes health prevents us from working as long as expected, or even company closures, amalgamations, and bankruptcies may jeopardize the continuity of work. Since our life spans are increasing, and we're living longer, some of us may have to take care of ageing parents and take some time off work or reduce our work schedules. I would think many of us may very well have been affected by one or more of these situations. For these reasons alone, financial security in retirement could be challenging.

David Chilton reminds us in The Wealthy Barber, "There are a couple major expenditures that sometimes arise in retirement that can be very costly, very difficult to cope with on a pension, even a good pension. Sadly, deteriorating health goes hand in hand with advancing age. There are any number of medical costs that can cause your financial health to decline right along with your physical health. And yes, admittedly you will probably no longer have dependent children, but what about dependent parents? As I've said many times, Canadians are, for the most part, financial illiterates."

My suggestion to those of you wanting to retire from your full-time job would be to continue to work on a part-time basis as long as you can, providing you have the energy and good health to be able to do so. Ideally, it would be a fun job and more than likely very different from what you may have been working at full-time. Or you may be in a position to do some consulting work in an area you are well skilled at and like but in a more flexible environment with fewer hours. The flexibility is wonderful and even better if you're able to supplement your income. Having said that, you will need to be careful with taxes. I will talk a little more about taxes in my next chapter.

More important than anything is that you take good care of yourself so you will be able to retire while you are healthy and enjoy many years of retirement. I had a good long-time friend who retired at a relatively young age of 53, with 30-plus pensionable years accumulated right out of high school. She enjoyed some time at home before she realized retirement was indeed expensive. She went back to work for another five years in a job she liked and at the same time was able to supplement her pension. Tragically, when she was in her early 60s, she became ill and passed away before her 65th birthday. Unfortunately, she never lived to collect her Old Age Security (OAS). Sadly, my very dear friend whom I mourn to this day worried every day about her finances in retirement. I recall her saying to me more than once that there wasn't a day that went by when she didn't think (or worry) over her finances. I never really understood that, and I would question her, but she would remind me that because I was still working, my situation was very different. I was not on the fixed income that she was. I was phasing into retirement and had the opportunity to reduce my status to working four days a week. It is only now I'm retired that I can identify with her feelings. Regrettably, she is no longer here, and I am unable to share that anxiety with her.

Chapter 2
RRSPS IN RETIREMENT

SOME OF YOU MAY HAVE INVESTED IN RRSPS WHILE WORKING full-time providing you were earning a better-than-average wage. If not, the tax benefit may not have benefitted you significantly. Even so, if your wage was not a good one, chances are you would not have found the money at the end of the day to invest at all. However, if you were lucky enough to have earned a good wage and were able to contribute to RSPs to reduce your taxable income, chances are you would have received a nice refund once you submitted your taxes for that year. And if you did, even better if you were able to put that refund to good use. It's a nice tax-saving tool and one that you will clearly appreciate upon retirement, providing you leave the money invested until you do. You do not want to draw the funds while you're still working full-time because of the increased taxes when you withdraw. As you know, it is intended to supplement your reduced income in retirement when you are in a lower taxable income bracket. Having said that, I suppose if you unexpectedly became unemployed and suddenly brought in less money, you may have had to draw from your RRSPs. Not the ideal situation, but if there are no other resources to take from, then the RRSP withdrawal may be the only recourse.

RRSPs, TFSAs, possibly a company pension, other investments, CPP, and OAS will provide you with your income in retirement. Your RRSP can be converted to a Register Retirement Income Fund (RRIF) at any time until age 71, which is the maximum, to provide you with a regular monthly income. Ideally, you will not have a mortgage or any other debt or dependents. The latter may not be true for some and may come with challenges. Everyone's situation is different, and we each need to manage accordingly, whatever that might be. I know of several people who have retired with mortgages and personal lines of credit (PLC). You may have the retirement income to manage that expense, as I expect many do. However, if you find you need to take more from your RRSPs on a regular basis, the taxes can really hurt you, sometimes as much as 30 percent or more depending on your tax bracket and the amount you withdraw in that year. The problem is that in your retiring years, an RRSP fund (or RRIF if already converted) will not provide you with the financial returns you may be accustomed to because of the low interest rates, particularly for two reasons: you are not getting the return on investment since the financial collapse in 2007, and more than likely your RRSP or RRIF is now invested conservatively because of age. If you can see a return of 6-7 percent in today's market, I think that's respectable. I wonder if we had not had to endure the pain of the financial collapse, we may have been able to see double-digit returns. Awe. The gloom of it all.

Simply, if you find yourself having to withdraw more than the maximum amount, I would think it would be better to find that part-time work I mentioned above, providing of course health and circumstances permit, to supplement your retirement income to enable you to reduce the amount withdrawn from your RRSPs. I should have done that a few years back after there was no more work for me at the Hamilton Health Sciences Centre, where I worked with my group after retiring from McMaster University. At that time, my granddaughter came along, and I chose to help out with childcare part-time. I knew I could not do that and take on another job as well. It's all about priorities. We have to accept them for the options that are available at that time. There's no point in beating ourselves up over decisions that were made several years ago. There are reasons why we choose to do what we do at the time. We need to be grateful we have the means to make these choices.

RRSPs are cashed in immediately upon death and are included in your income and taxed based on last year's taxation rate. It would be wise to have beneficiaries named in your RRSP, and depending upon your rate of taxation upon death, your beneficiaries may feel they have to absorb all those taxes. Rest assured the RRSP is primarily for you in your retirement years. Most in today's economy may very well use up all of their funds in that time, I would think those beneficiaries can only be elated if there is in fact anything left at all. TFSA withdrawals, however, are tax-free since the contributions were made with after-tax dollars. While some may not agree with an insurance policy, if you are able to take out a term policy at a preferred rate, providing you are healthy enough to do that, you might want to consider that to protect your assets. If anything, the policy may help to reduce some taxation and any lingering expenses or debt.

Chapter 3
HOUSING

FOR THOSE OF YOU WHO MAY HAVE BEEN LUCKY ENOUGH TO HAVE benefitted from the recent housing bubble and were able to sell your home well above the asking price, maybe even with a bidding war, kudos to you. If you just so happen to be one of the fortunate ones and better still if you were downsizing at the same time, you may have realized a hefty profit and been able to nicely contribute to your nest egg. Until recently, the housing market has been crazy and incredibly scary at the same time. When it was going to end was the concern for many. The Toronto prices were outrageous and pushing the prices in Hamilton to record high values. We all knew it couldn't continue forever, but when was the bubble ever going to break? Vancouver house prices have always been higher until the BC government implemented the foreign investment tax on homebuyers.

Recently the Ontario government did the same thing to cool Toronto's hot housing market. Today I heard on the radio that Toronto housing sales are down 35 percent. This has had a similar effect in Hamilton and surrounding areas as well. The Bank of Canada increased the interest rate by a quarter of a point after record low rates for a number of years and just today increased it again to 1 percent. Of late I have been seeing a lot of For Sale signs on many properties, and I expect they too are hoping to get a piece of the action. However, my thinking is they may be too late. It all boils down to supply and demand. It is now a buyers' market for those interested in buying.

In David Chilton's book The Wealthy Barber, he states, "Aging adults who voluntarily sell and then move to an apartment or old folks' home are few and far between. In most instances, people die still owning their home. So in a way, they haven't benefited from their homes' increased value." Interesting, and yet I expect they may have lived rent-free for a number of years, and hopefully they have children to leave it to as inheritance. For those renting, and now particularly because of the recent housing boom, rents also have increased substantially. Very seldom do they come down. For those who may want to move and scale down to an even smaller one-bedroom apartment, it may cost more than what you are paying now. That's tough on a retiree on a fixed income. Through no fault of our own, we as retirees are now faced with increased housing costs and rents, and these are the major costs due to inflation. It is true with utilities and food as well as almost every other commodity you can think of. The prices never come down. While the housing bubble may be over for now, the market values have only stabilized. They still remain higher than ever. Back in the early 2000s, I may have seriously considered buying a condo apartment. Today I can't even think about it. I know back in 2007 I sold my parents' home for $169,000. In today's market, I expect it would go for possibly more than $350,000. Should have held on to it. Hindsight is wonderful.

For a retiree, the housing accommodations have become increasingly challenging. If we are lucky enough to have money invested in the financial markets, chances are we are not seeing the gains that have been realized in the past. We're not making money or earning money, and what money we do have is very much consumed through inflation and taxes. Our financial resources are not unlimited, and so my big concern is simply this: Can we continue to live in a safe and clean environment independently while we remain healthy? Many are living well into their 90s as they watch their resources become depleted, and seemingly there is no easy recourse. On a brighter note, providing you are financially able to live independently until your health no longer permits, you may very well qualify for a nursing home, but only if there is *availability*.

In The Ultimate Money Guide for Canadians, Jerry White states, "As government debt grows, personal income taxes will continue to rise and prevent Canadians from being able to accumulate enough wealth to look after themselves in their later years." I have always maintained that as Canadians both taxes and inflation are huge detriments for many. Having said that, we need to find creative strategies to hold on to our finances to maintain a level of security and comfort in our retiring years. I'm still working on that. If and when I ever do find a solution, possibly I can share that with you.

Chapter 4
THE FINANCIAL COLLAPSE IN 2008

"THERE IS ENOUGH MONEY IN THE WORLD FOR EVERYONE'S NEED, but not for everyone's greed," states Frank Buchman in Bubbles, Bankers & Bailouts. Who would have thought a few scammers on Wall Street had the power and means to collapse the entire global economy just ten years ago. This is criminal and inhumane, and yet so many big companies crumbled before our very eyes, not to mention the number of innocent people worldwide affected by it all. How does the average person prepare for such an impact? I realize it's all very relative, and we have each been affected in many different ways. In the United States, states such as Arizona and Florida have been heavily impacted, and many became homeless. The financial markets crashed, and while many lost their homes, many may have even lost their lifetime savings. So tragic, due to a few very greedy and callous individuals on Wall Street. And how do we recover from such a tragedy?

In November 2008, then Canadian Prime Minister Stephen Harper stated, "The financial crisis has become an economic crisis, and the world is entering an economic period unlike, and potentially as dangerous as, anything we have faced since 1929." While many have lost homes and retirement savings, we continue to strive to recover from such an atrocity. We really have no choice but to weather the storm and hope that over time some of our losses may be recovered. Although for us baby boomers, there may not be enough time for that, and I think many of us may have already figured that out. We are beyond our working years and now living off our pensions, savings, and investments. Thankfully our children and grandchildren may have enough time to build their wealth and power while they are still active in the workforce.

Several banks in the United States collapsed and may not ever recover. We have to be thankful for our banks in Canada in that they were able to survive the collapse.

The World Economic Forum ranked Canada's banking system the best in the world, according to John Reynolds in Bubbles, Bankers & Bailouts. He goes on to say that the "U.S. banks are subject to much tighter regulation and favoured small locally owned banks and fewer branches creating a competitive but an unstable system. Canadian banks expanded nationally thereby producing a broader and more stable foundation that allowed them to ride out difficult times." This is another positive to be thankful for if you are Canadian and living in Canada. During this time credit may have become a lot tighter if you needed to borrow, but it is comforting to know our banks are viable with "total assets of about 2.5 trillion and the largest five Canadian banks are consistently rated by Forbes magazine among the top two hundred banks in the world," as paraphrased by John Reynolds in Bubbles, Bankers & Bailouts.

Many of us may curse the Canadian banks from time to time because of à la carte expensing and record profits, and recently they have appeared in the media suggesting they are not always looking out for our best interests. Agreed, they may operate aggressively, but without their stability, the financial collapse of 2008 may have been far more devastating for many. So shout out to our Canadian banks; they too need to be commended on occasion.

Chapter 5
RECOVERY AFTER 10 YEARS

I DON'T KNOW THAT WE HAVE RECOVERED FROM THE GLOBAL financial collapse of 2007-08. Yes, the stock markets may have recovered and people are spending lots of money, but economic statistics must not have shown the strength until recently when the Bank of Canada finally raised the borrowing rate to 1 percent. The unemployment rate has stabilized, yet there are many young people trapped in service-sector jobs making no more than minimum wage. You cannot exist on minimum wage unless you're living at home with Mom and Dad. Household debts are at an all time high. Why? The cost of securing a mortgage has been at record low borrowing rates following the financial demise. Families have been able to manage huge mortgages because of this, but as we see the interest rates slowly increasing, when mortgages come up for renewal, this could have a huge impact on the family budget. In a way one might think with interest rates at an all-time low now for so long, a false sense of security may have dominated the average family.

In the same way that our now federal Liberal government is investing millions into the economy, it's very much similar to the Bank of Canada policy. My thinking is that huge amounts of credit circulating globally are keeping our economy afloat. Without the credit available to so many people, there wouldn't be the same amount of money circulating to support all the businesses and commodities. The amount of credit is driving the prices up because of the *availability of credit* and not necessarily because of the *availability of cash.* If we were to have to dip into our pockets to pay cash for the majority of items we want or need, we may think twice before we make the purchase or spend less. I too am guilty of that, although I use my debit card the majority of time, which ultimately gets me into less trouble.

This abundance and availability of credit only pushes demand and ultimately the rate of inflation up. "Current inflation Canada (CPI Canada)—the inflation is based upon the Canadian consumer price index. The index is a measure of the average price, which consumers spend on a market-based 'basket' of goods and services. Inflation based upon the consumer price index (CPI) is the main inflation indicator in most countries," says the Inflation. eu website, which reports worldwide inflation data. In July 2017, inflation was reported as 1.2 percent (see Table 1). Really? Are all commodities factored into that? Why does it cost so much to live? Table 1 is the Canadian CPI Basket of Goods and Services from Statistics Canada, which shows the goods and services used to factor the inflation rate.

Demand is what drives up the rate of inflation, and prices will continue to inflate if we continue to spend. Eliminating the credit would be an interesting scenario to see just how well the economy would survive then. It would more than likely collapse, and then we would be in a deep recession or even depression. So what is the answer? Spend less, save more. I know, that's boring, but it's safe. If fewer people refused to pay the exorbitant cable rates, then those rates just might drop to a fairer rate. Why don't these cable companies offer a seniors' rate, anyway?

Canadian CPI Basket of Goods and Services

This is the content of the basket of goods and services that the Canadian government (Statistics Canada) uses to generate the Consumer Price Index (CPI) and inflation rates. Next to each item you will see the weight (out of 100) assigned to it based on the average Canadian's spending. Note that both the content of the basket and the weight of each component were updated in 2015. The basket's content is updated every four years, and the weights are updated every two years.

Table 1 shows the evolution of the weight of each basket category from 1986 to 2015.

Table 1: Average Canadian's Spending by Category (% of wallet)

Component	1986	1992	1996	2001	2005	2009	2011	2013	2015
Food	18.1	18.0	17.8	16.8	16.9	16.1	16.35	16.6	16.4
Shelter	25.7	27.6	27.1	26.3	25.7	27.5	25.9	26.3	26.8
Household Operations, Furnishings and Equipment	10.7	10.4	10.7	11.1	11.4	11.8	12.6	12.7	13.1
Clothing and Footwear	8.7	6.8	6.3	6.0	5.6	5.6	6.2	5.8	6.1
Transportation	18.3	17.2	18.6	19.4	19.6	19.3	20.0	20.0	19.1
Health and Personal Care	4.2	4.4	4.6	4.6	4.8	5.0	4.9	4.9	4.7
Recreation, Education and Reading	8.8	10.2	11.3	12.5	13.0	11.8	11.2	11.0	10.9
Alcoholic Beverages and Tobacco Products	5.6	5.5	3.5	3.3	3.1	3.0	2.8	2.8	2.9

Components may not add up to 100 due to rounding.

Looking at Table 1, you can clearly see that housing/shelter, at 26.8 percent in 2015, had the highest inflation index, and followed by transportation and food at 19.1 and 16.4, respectively. Those three main components alone add up to 62.3 percent. As for food, I find it surprising to see that the index fell from 18.1 in 1986 to 16.4 in 2015. I would have thought it would have been the other way around. It's difficult to believe the cost of food actually dropped in 2015. I wonder how many of us even realize that.

Chapter 6
FINANCIAL MARKETS NOW

I AM NOT CONVINCED WE HAVE REALLY RECOVERED FROM THE devastating collapse of 2007-08. I think many lost a lot of money or jobs because of it, and I still believe the economy is quite fragile. These are challenging times, and while there appears to have been much recovery in the past few years, I wonder where some of us might be had there not been the financial demise. I suppose we will never know the answer to that, and I expect it's a good thing we don't. I also think the inflation rates would be a lot higher than what we have seen, although I cannot imagine. There are too many factors for me, at least, to analyze it too much.

In Table 2, according to Canada Inflation Rate, 1915-2017 Data, Canada's inflation rate "averaged 3.15 percent from 1915 until 2017, reaching an all time high of 21.60 percent in June of 1920 and a record low of -17.80 percent in June of 1921." When we look at the table we can clearly see that the inflation rate has been well controlled at an average of 3.15 percent now for 100 years, and clearly over the last couple of years, from August 2016 at 1.1 to this past July at 1.2 percent. The table shows the rate spiked a bit early in January 2017 to 2.1 and then continued to drop. While we would never want to see the all-time high ever again in our lifetime, that of 21.60 percent in 1920, and now a low inflation rate of 1.2, many of us may be asking why everything is seemingly so expensive and why household debts are at an all-time high. Can we understand this, and more importantly now that I'm writing about it, can I understand it enough to even write about it? Nope, hence the citation below from an article on Global News from May 2017.

"Canadians often marvel at the fact that inflation remains stubbornly subdued despite the fact that life seems more and more expensive. Economists, too, have been wondering why one of the country's leading measures of price levels, the Consumer Price Index compiled by Statistics Canada, continues to show such lacklustre growth when the economy is healthy, unemployment is low and the Canadian dollar is weak" according to Global News, May 25, 2017. In that same article, it goes on to report "On Tuesday, National Bank suggested in a research note that the trouble might lie in StatsCan's method for tracking so-called shelter costs, the portion of income that Canadian households spend to keep a roof of their heads — whether it's home ownership costs or rent".

"This heavyweight component of the CPI (27 per cent of the index) is currently growing an anemic 2.2 per cent annually compared to a more robust 2.7 per cent for all other services," wrote National Bank economists Stefane Marion and Matthieu Arseneau. "They also noted rent inflation averages near a record low of one per cent in Toronto, Montreal and Vancouver. And that's despite the fact that headlines about doubling rents in Toronto recently prompted the Ontario government to boost rent controls in the province". "Bottom-line: Shelter cost inflation reported in the Canadian CPI report is eerily low," the National Bank report concludes.

So, does Canada's official inflation estimate really underplay housing costs? StatsCan told Global News "it doesn't believe CPI "significantly" underestimates shelter costs". And that none of that affects the inflation measure in a significant way, because CPI is more focused on tracking how much it costs to own or rent a home, rather than what it takes to buy one, director of consumer prices division,

Richard Evans, told Global News. And with mortgage rates so low, the cost of owning a home is at record lows.

On rents, the statistics bureau said it relies on data from the Labour Force Survey. The measure records the prices of rents by following a sample of renters through a period of five months. Every month, a new sub-section of renters (equal to one-sixth of the sample) is added to the group and an equally-sized batch is rotated out. This method has worked well in the past, said Evans, but the agency has started noticing its index is trending lower compared to other rent indexes. The statistics bureau is "investigating other data sources to supplement its current measure of rents and track rent changes over a longer period of time."

Still, if you expect any of the new measures to significantly drive up the official measure of inflation, you'll probably be disappointed. StatsCan doesn't anticipate any meaningful variations. If anything, it told Global News, its CPI measure tends to overestimate the cost of food, as it can't track in real time how Canadians change their shopping habits in response to price trends, by swapping out of their carts rapidly appreciating items in favour of cheaper goods. (This is a shortcoming of CPI measures in general, not just Canada's.) Frustrated prospective home-buyers might just have to accept the fact that the inflation index will never be a reflection of their plight.

Clear as mud. Right. Rather than try to explain in my own rambling words, I copied direct excerpts from the article in the hope that you, my readers, can better understand it, if it happens to interest you at all. I found the article to be interesting, and I think the final statement above sums it up rather eloquently. The three major components for shelter, food, and transportation have consistently over time shown high inflation, and they alone consume much of our after-tax dollars.

In spite of our overall low inflation rate increases, the interest rates remain low for mortgages but unfortunately for savings accounts as well. The financial markets may appear to have recovered, but clearly, as a retiree, if you are hoping to see any real gains on your investment, particularly if you need to draw from these funds, it is difficult to realize any significant growth. I continue to believe our economy remains fragile. There sure is a lot of credit circulating among consumers providing a false sense of security possibly to many. In spite of some who may enjoy a high wage, I expect much of the younger generation as well as many seniors are finding the cost of living to be extremely high. We pay a lot in taxes, and these will only continue to increase. Wages have not increased and have not kept up with inflation, and gone are the days when we can expect double-digit returns on our investments.

Table 2: Canada Inflation Rate

1915-2017 | Data | Chart | Calendar | Forecast

Consumer prices in Canada increased 1.2 percent year-on-year in July of 2017, higher than a 1 percent rise in June and in line with market expectations. Transportation and shelter cost made the highest upward contributions while prices of household operations, furnishings and equipment and clothing and footwear fell. Inflation Rate in Canada averaged 3.15 percent from 1915 until 2017, reaching an all time high of 21.60 percent in June of 1920 and a record low of -17.80 percent in June of 1921

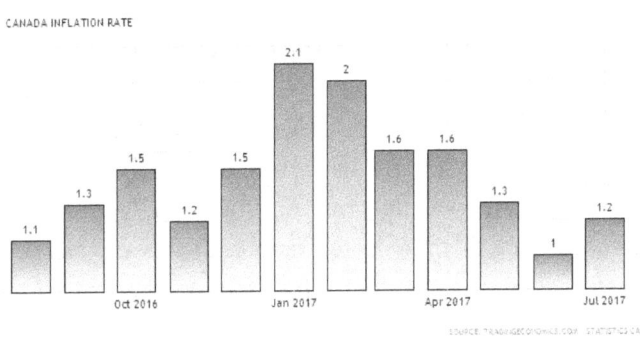

Chapter 7
SENIOR HELPING SENIORS

I SPENT A LOT OF TIME CARING FOR MY ELDERLY PARENTS AS THEY moved into their golden years. It was then that I began to realize the amount of help they required from time to time. Daily tasks both in the house and outside the home were becoming increasingly onerous for them. Coordinating and driving them to doctors' appointments and any other issues that may have come up all too soon became routine for me. Seniors are so proud. They strive to maintain their independence as long as they can and continue until it's painfully impossible. At least, that's the way it was for my parents, and now that I am a *younger* senior, I can better appreciate that reality. I often reflect upon what I remember my parents doing or not doing, and it is now that I can truly respect their needs at that time in their lives.

Very soon after I retired, I developed a passion to help seniors. There is a tremendous need out there, and over time I have realized two things: (1) Seniors do not want to admit to growing old and feeling incapable of doing the things they have always been able to do in the past, which translates to striving to maintain their independence; and (2) they may not actually have the means or funds to pay for the help they may eventually admit to needing. Many of them are so proud (some may be stubborn), but I would like to think it's more pride than the latter. For these reasons alone, it's a difficult service to tap into, unless of course you choose to be aggressive, and that I am not. Although I always knew I wasn't about to embark on another career path, I wanted to put myself out there in a friendly but professional way to let people around me know this is a passion I feel a need to do.

Through word of mouth only, I now have a few clients I work with in a variety of ways, and I find it to be one of the most rewarding challenges I have ever found myself doing. It is occasionally frustrating, I have to admit, but that's to be expected with anything. It's never a perfect bed of roses. There will always be bumps along the way, but for the most part, I feel a tremendous sense of satisfaction after spending time with any one of them. I volunteer a lot of my time, although I do charge a reasonable fee for specific tasks they might ask for simply because I value my time, knowing very well this will never make me rich. What has developed is a friendship and companionship, and they each call me regularly, often just to chat, knowing I will listen. It's difficult to bill for that service. I'm not a lawyer or doctor, so how could I possibly bill for a phone call from a client (and friend, in most cases) just needing to talk?

As a senior, I firmly believe we need to keep ourselves busy with whatever makes us happy. For the most part, we are in our last phase of life, and we need to make the best of it. There's no turning back, and there's not a lot of time left to make too many mistakes. This is the time to engage in things that you might have put off in the past because of time constraints with career and a growing family. That is no longer the case in retirement. For all the recent retirees out there or those planning to retire soon, think wisely about how you choose to spend your time. I think often too much time is spent over our financial well-being and not enough on our social well-being. However, I am realizing that our overall health, both physical and emotional, is equally as important, or even more. Having said that, our primary focus is to remain healthy as long as we can to provide us with the independence to do the types of things that will contribute to longevity and a good quality of life for the majority of our retirement years.

Chapter 8
SENIOR HOUSING FACILITIES

"IT'S IMPORTANT TO BE ABLE TO LIVE WITHOUT A LOT OF MONEY because having a lot of money doesn't make you important," says Sandra Foster in You Can't Take It With You: Common-Sense Estate Planning for Canadians (5th edition). Yet one might ask if there will be enough money to be able to go into a retirement home or nursing home, if need be. Will there be enough to meet all the requirements in retirement? How much is too much? How much is a "lot of money"? I think the way things are going I would rather feel the security of having "a lot of money." I don't need to feel important. I simply need to feel secure. Whatever I don't use I will happily leave to my kids. That is my plan.

If you are unable to continue to live independently in your home, there remains the concern for availability in senior accommodations, whether a retirement home or nursing home, if and when the time comes. I think there may be more options for a retirement home accommodation if you have lots of money. I know that some of the newer complexes can cost as much as $4000 to $5000 a month in rent. For a senior couple with a combined retirement income that may be feasible, but if you are a woman living alone, that just might take a big chunk of your monthly income. If you have a home to sell, then proceeds from the sale can help with the increased rent. With having to pay that amount, there will be amenities included and possibly a food plan. If you are ready for that lifestyle and can afford it, kudos to you. I'm not so sure just how many can.

"Statistics show that many Canadians retire near—or under—the poverty level. In fact, it's said that over 50 percent of retired Canadians need some form of government assistance to survive", according to David Chilton in The Wealthy Barber. He goes on to say, "That such a situation exists in a country enjoying our level of economic prosperity is nothing short of embarrassing. Nowhere is Canadians' lack of financial acumen more glaringly evident. With our aging population and the fact that many experts now question the long-term stability of the CPP, it's more important now than ever for Canadians to save properly for their 'golden years.'" For those of us already into our "golden years," there really isn't a lot we can change but simply ride the wave as best we can with the resources we have. We can educate our children and grandchildren to save as best they can to hopefully help them prepare well for their retirement years.

Some of you may be able to live in your home independently for many years into retirement. If you do happen to qualify for a nursing home, I know many may believe they cannot afford a nursing home, but that is not true. If you don't care to have a semi-private or private room, there is a subsidy available if you are unable to afford the cost. I know that many of the nursing homes have been mandated by the government to update their facilities; the basic room now is really not that different from the semi-private (at least this is true at Wentworth Lodge in Dundas, Ontario, where updates were completed in 2007). I can speak from experience because I had both my parents there. While my mother was in a semi-private, my dad preferred a private room. Fortunately for them, they had the funds to support their wishes. My mother for the most part was a stay-at-home parent and would have otherwise qualified for subsidy. Your assets are not a consideration for a subsidy for a rate reduction. It is based on your personal income tax return alone, unless that has changed since 2007.

Below I have copied directly from the Ontario Government website on long-term care homes to show the eligibility criteria and the rates for a long-term facility.

Eligibility

To live in a long-term care home, you must:

- be age 18 or older
- have a valid Ontario Health Insurance Program (OHIP) card
- have care needs including:
- 24-hours nursing care and personal care
- frequent assistance with activities of daily living
- on-site supervision or monitoring to ensure your safety or well-being
- have care needs which cannot be safely met in the community though publicly-funded community-based services and other care-giving support
- have care needs which can be met in a long-term care home

Costs

All personal and nursing care provided by long-term care homes in Ontario are funded by the government. You must pay for accommodation charges such as room and board.

Accommodation costs are set by the Ministry of Health and Long-Term Care and are standard in all long-term care homes across Ontario. The current (maximum) rates are:

	Daily rate	Monthly rate
Long-stay Basic1	$ 59.82	$1,819
Long-stay Semi-private2	$72.12 (Basic plus a maximum of $12.30)	$2,193
Long-stay Private2	$85.45 (Basic plus a maximum of $25.63)	$2,599
Short-stay	$38.72	N/A

Government subsidy

If you don't have enough income to pay for the basic room, you may be eligible for a subsidy. This is known as a rate reduction. The subsidy is not available to people requesting semi-private or private rooms. If you qualify, you or a lawful representative must complete an application form and submit it to your long-term care home.

Chapter 9
FINDING BALANCE

OFTEN I FIND THERE IS TOO MUCH FOCUS AND ENERGY PLACED ON how much money we have (or not) and our everyday expenses. True, the cost of living is high, and unless you have a ton of money, that most likely is not about to change. We need to prioritize our needs and wants and budget accordingly—more than ever in our retirement years. It's a constant challenge, and one wonders when and if that will ever go away. Well, it may if you win the lottery or happen to inherit a nice sum of money. There are pros and cons to that as well.

If you win the lottery, you may suddenly appear to have gained a few more friends who land on your doorstep, and very quickly your life turns around. If you're kindhearted and overly generous, you might be left with little, depending of course on the amount of the windfall. For me, since I am a little more generous than what I possibly should be, more than likely I would use up all my money and be back in the financial position I started from. *Maybe.*

In retirement, ideally we should not have to worry about our health and finances. Hopefully we have prepared ourselves well for this phase of life. We may not have been thinking about retirement in our twenties, but by the time we have reached our forties, I think many of us have become increasingly aware of just how much we might need and what we need to do to achieve it. How does anybody really know just how much we will need? David Chilton in The Wealthy Barber writes, "If the decline in expenses happened to coincide perfectly with the date of retirement instead of occurring earlier, I don't believe there would be a major problem. But it seldom does. Adjusting to a fairly dramatic drop in your disposable income is not my idea of a good way to start retired life. Especially since it's a myth that present-day retired people spend much less money on lifestyle than their working counterparts. People don't retire and head straight to the rocking chair. While the rest of us are slaving away, many retirees are playing golf, taking up hobbies, travelling extensively, and participating in a myriad of other activities that all have one common denominator—they cost money!"

So there you have it. I can clearly vouch for those statements. Among my circle of retired friends, and thankfully most of us are relatively healthy, we most definitely have not retired to our rocking chairs. We are all very active and enjoying life. In our earlier years, we have no idea how important it is to look after ourselves to prepare us for our golden years. We have all heard the phrase "old age is not for the weak and mild," and as I'm approaching my seventieth year, I am reminded of just that. It is imperative to keep moving. We are living longer, and we need to take care of both our health and finances in order to maintain our independence as long as we can.

I firmly believe in regular exercise, whatever that may entail for you, and generally live a healthy lifestyle. Ideally, eat a well-balanced diet, do moderate to regular exercise, and, if you feel so inclined, drink a glass of wine or two a day, and no smoking. Never any guarantees, but at least you can be comforted in knowing you have done your best in the hope to be in good shape to battle whatever challenges you might have to endure. We refer to the last chapter of life as "our golden years". Not so "golden" I often hear from those who may have some challenging health issues.

Chapter 10
WHAT'S REALLY IMPORTANT?

FOR ME, MY FAMILY AND CLOSE FRIENDS ARE INVALUABLE TO MY well-being, without a doubt. My overall health and the health of my kids, grandkids, and immediate family are more important to me than anything. Without the comfort of knowing my kids are healthy and that I have my immediate family and a few very great long-time friends to share my life with, I am afraid my life may otherwise be rather dismal, to say the least. No amount of money could ever replace these gifts. To be taken for breakfast by my 17-year-old grandson when I least expect is truly quite gratifying. So thoughtful, and only because he was able to use my car to obtain his driver's license. And when I say my six-year old granddaughter runs up to me and throws her arms around me in apparent jubilance because Grandma came to pick her up from school may sound like a small feat, yet these special moments I will remember and treasure for life.

Every day we hear of natural disasters where families have to flee their homes with literally the clothes on their backs. If you have never been faced with that type of tragedy, you should feel extremely fortunate. Major hurricanes, tornadoes, earthquakes, forest fires, and all the after effects associated with such disasters is an overwhelming event many of us may never have to face, hopefully. Unfortunately, we are not immune to these catastrophic events since the media continues to remind us daily of the impact of global warming. I personally feel blessed every day I watch the news when I hear of yet another tragedy. We are so lucky to live in this region where, although we do have our share of misfortunes, I truly believe we live in the best part of the world. Our lives could be particularly more difficult and possibly devastating in many other parts of the world. I do feel blessed.

It really is the simpler aspects of life that help us to stay focused and happy. Today there seems to be so much interest and attention to finances and commodities. True, we need money to pay for our immediate needs like food, shelter, and clothing, but beyond that, do we really need all this other stuff we so often spend our money on? You just have to look around to see the amount of money spent on electronics. We have become addicted to technology, and we are forever feeling compelled to upgrade or replace our computers, cell phones, and tablets and all the other devices that continue to become obsolete. This will not change unless the costs and consequences become debilitating, so we have to find some balance and control before there is a major problem.

Today's technology cannot replace the good relationships we make with the people who truly matter in our lives. It may be more difficult for the younger generation to realize that because they have grown up with the technology. My generation has become quite obsessed with it as well, although I think we may be a little more cognizant of the implications that may emerge. I often think we need to get back to basics and strive to keep an element of simplicity in our lives. Life can get quite complicated if we allow it to. Building and maintaining active and healthy lifestyles and relationships with friends and family are imperative to our overall health and happiness. Things or stuff, whether a new sports car or the latest in technology, are not tangible possessions. Sure, they may be fun to have, but they clearly are not required to sustain our overall happiness.

Just recently, I started to read the book Living the Good Life by David Patchell-Evans, the owner of GoodLife

Fitness. What an inspiring book, and I have only just begun the read, but if I may quote him directly: "There isn't a medication you can buy, or a car or a house, or a trip that will make you feel the way you do when your body is fit and healthy." Yet another reminder to keep moving and to do whatever it takes to keep our minds, souls, and bodies healthy and fit.

Financial Survival, published by McMaster University, lists the six powers of success as noted below and reports, "All of our corporate seminars and workshops emphasize setting goals that require a balanced approach to successful financial and lifestyle planning. Many people have enjoyed tremendous financial success but at the expense of poor health and a breakdown in family and personal relationships." Note that physical health and wellness is number one at the top of the list, and this publication states, "If you haven't got your physical health, it doesn't matter what else is going on in your life because you'll find it difficult to enjoy if you're uncomfortable and in a lot of pain or discomfort." I couldn't agree more. Note that "precious relationships" follows as the second priority to success.

1. Physical health and wellness
2. Precious relationships
3. Personal growth
4. Profession/career/vocation

5. Personal fulfillment
6. Pursuit of financial freedom

We cannot allow ourselves to forget the basic necessities in life: food, water, air, shelter, and clothing. Personally, I panic at the very thought of not having clean drinking water alone; we are often reminded that many in developing countries are without. If we look around our immediate surroundings, we really do have much more than that. Yet one might ask how important these other things are and how much they contribute to our overall happiness and well-being. Probably not a lot. I think we just have to remind ourselves about what I wrote earlier, taken from You Can't Take It with You by Sandra E. Foster: "It's important to be able to live without a lot of money because having a lot of money doesn't make you important." More than ever in today's economy and particularly in retirement, that seemingly may be the mentality we need to develop since retirement will undoubtedly consume much of our hard-earned savings and investments over time. It may be even more prevalent than ever to see many in our generations outlive their money, now that we are living longer, particularly females. Will our government be prepared to maintain us as we live well into our nineties and have used up all our financial resources? That's a scary scenario I am not about to delve into.

An article I read in the Hamilton Spectator in October 2017 notes, "Experts say women need to save a bigger chunk of their income for retirement than men because they get paid less and live longer than average." That same article says, "Women always worry running out of money and being a bag woman on the streets. That said, the average woman is often not as well positioned as the average man for retirement. While part of that may be by choice in choosing to stay home to take care of kids or leaving work early to take care of parents who are unwell and or elderly." Moreover, "Pressure for these women is extremely elevated, more so for women who don't have a partner to share housing expenses for the rest of their lives or had additional retirement savings."

When I read the article, I felt the author was personally writing to me since I was one of many to choose to stay home when my kids were young and later to take care of my aging parents. So brace yourself, my female readers. We really need to be astute about our finances and manage well throughout our lifespan, knowing very well it could be a long one. Having said that, realistically, we can only do what we can do, including taking care of today, because tomorrow remains uncertain. We cannot forget the important realities of life regardless—namely our physical and mental health and the important people in our lives. By that I mean, and if I may repeat, family and good friends will always be the glue to help keep our lives in perspective.

David Chilton in The Wealthy Barber states, "Your years in retirement should be among the best years of your life. So you owe it to yourself to do everything possible now to enable you to enjoy fully those later years. That means saving enough money in your working years to enable you to maintain your income in retirement." My children, I can only hope, will thank me when I'm gone because I am continually looking at ways to simplify my life. I realize what makes me happy, and once you know what's important, it is so much easier to declutter your life. I am on a mission to do just that. I find it to be extremely cathartic, and my hope is that my kids might appreciate the fact that there may be very little left to toss, with the exception of a few memorabilia I hope they will treasure. I hope you too can find some pleasure in that mind-set. Happy retirement, my friends.

Live well, love much, and laugh often.

REFERENCES

7. John Lawrence Reynolds, *Bubbles Bankers, & Bailouts.*
8. David Chilton, *The Wealthy Barber.*
9. Jerry White, *The Ultimate Money Guide for Canadians.*
10. Sandra E. Foster, *You Can't Take It with You. Common-Sense Estate Planning for Canadians (5th edition).*
11. *Hamilton Spectator,* October 2017.
12. *Global News,* May 2017.
13. Ontario Government website.
14. RetirementAdvisor.ca website.
15. Inflation.eu website.
16. Statistics Canada website.
17. Canada Inflation Rate, 1915-2017 Data.
18. David Patchell-Evans, *Living the Good Life.*
19. McMaster University, *Financial Survival for the 21st Century (5th revised edition)*

GLOSSARY

* CPP Canada Pension Plan
* DPP Defined Pension Plan
* HHSC Hamilton Health Sciences Centre
* OAS Old Age Security
* PLC Personal line of credit
* RRIF Registered Retired Income Fund
* RRSP Registered Retirement Savings Plan
* TFSA Tax Free Savings Account

ABOUT THE AUTHOR

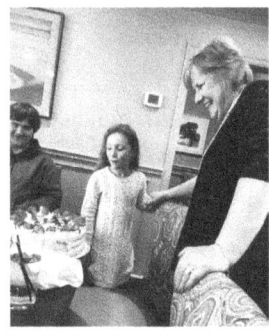

Wendy Yacura is a retired academic medical research assistant whose contributions to clinical trials have been recognized worldwide. She is a loving mother of two adult children, a grandmother of two, a loyal sister, and a dedicated friend and companion to countless people who love and respect her. She became a divorcee at the age of forty-five after almost twenty-five years of marriage and has been on her own now for the past twenty-five years. As a first-time author, although having written and distributed a few memoirs over the years, she never felt the need or urge to publish until now. She feels a compassion to share what she considers to be some of the myths and realities of retirement from her own perspective: that of a divorced woman having to face the challenges that retirement can sometimes present. She hopes to shed some light on issues such as finances and housing, and the impact of inflation and rising costs to those already in retirement and for those moving into retirement. She presents both facts and personal stories in hopes that those who are approaching their retirement years can take away some useful advice that may help in adjusting to this "new" way of life. Wendy's passion for helping others along with her determination and spirited nature combine to make her book a wise and down-to-earth read.

Lorrie Costantini

www.ingramcontent.com/pod-product-compliance
Lightning Source LLC
LaVergne TN
LVHW011858060526
838200LV00054B/4412